WOMEN IN THE OLYMPICS

BY HEATHER RULE

SportsZone

An Imprint of Abdo Publishing
abdopublishing.com

WOMEN IN SPORTS

abdopublishing.com

Published by Abdo Publishing, a division of ABDO, PO Box 398166, Minneapolis, Minnesota 55439. Copyright © 2018 by Abdo Consulting Group, Inc. International copyrights reserved in all countries. No part of this book may be reproduced in any form without written permission from the publisher. SportsZone™ is a trademark and logo of Abdo Publishing.

Printed in the United States of America, North Mankato, Minnesota
042017
092017

Cover Photo: Ron Heflin/AP Images
Interior Photos: Ron Heflin/AP Images, 1; Matt Dunham/AP Images, 4–5; AP Images, 6, 8, 12–13, 14, 18, 22, 25; Getty Images Sport/Getty Images, 11; Tony Triolo/Sports Illustrated/Getty Images, 17; Maze/AP Images, 21; Thomas Kienzle/AP Images, 26, 42; Pete Leabo/AP Images, 28; Susan Ragan/AP Images, 30–31; Andreas Altwein/picture-alliance/dpa/AP Images, 32; Doug Mills/AP Images, 34; David J. Phillip/AP Images, 37; Julio Cortez/AP Images, 38–39; Mark Humphrey/AP Images, 40; Jae C. Hong/AP Images, 45

Editor: Patrick Donnelly
Series Designer: Laura Polzin
Content Consultant: Rita Liberti, PhD, Professor of Kinesiology, California State University, East Bay

Publisher's Cataloging-in-Publication Data

Names: Rule, Heather, author.
Title: Women in the Olympics / by Heather Rule.
Description: Minneapolis, MN : Abdo Publishing, 2018. | Series: Women in sports | Includes bibliographical references and index.
Identifiers: LCCN 2016962120 | ISBN 9781532111594 (lib. bdg.) | ISBN 9781680789447 (ebook)
Subjects: LCSH: Athletes--Juvenile literature. | Women athletes--Juvenile literature. | Women Olympic athletes--Juvenile literature. | Olympics--Juvenile literature.
Classification: DDC 796--dc23
LC record available at http://lccn.loc.gov/2016962120

TABLE OF
CONTENTS

OLYMPIC PIONEERS

I t's hard to imagine the Olympics without female athletes. But that's how the modern Olympics started. Women were not allowed to participate in the first modern Games, held in Athens, Greece, in 1896. Four years later, 23 women were among the 1,224 competitors in Paris, France. The numbers grew steadily. The International Olympic Committee (IOC) said that 4,655 female athletes participated in the 2012 Summer Olympics in London, England. That's more than 44 percent of all competitors.

The Winter Olympics, which began in 1924, experienced a similar pattern. Just 13 of the 313 participants at the first Winter Games were women. That number grew to 1,105 women, approximately

Women comprised nearly half of the athletes at the 2012 Summer Games in London.

40 percent of the athletes at the 2014 Winter Games in Sochi, Russia.

The first women to win gold medals at the 1924 Winter Games were Austrians Helene Engelmann and Herma Planck-Szabo. Engelmann won for mixed pairs figure skating. Planck-Szabo won the figure skating gold.

With the increase in opportunities to compete came the first batch of female athletic stars. Norwegian figure skater Sonja Henie was 11 years old when she competed in the 1924 Winter Games in Chamonix, France. She finished last, but she didn't let that get her down. Henie came back to take the gold medal in 1928, 1932, and 1936. Henie remains the only woman to win three gold medals in singles figure skating.

Fanny Blankers-Koen was another early star. She was a track and field athlete from the Netherlands who set 16 world records in eight events. Blankers-Koen saved her best performances for the 1948 London Olympics, where she won gold medals in the 100- and 200-meter dashes, the 80-meter hurdles, and 4x100 relay. She might have won more, but at the time athletes could only compete in three individual events.

Fanny Blankers-Koen, *foreground*, clears the last hurdle in the 80-meter finals at the 1948 Summer Olympics in London.

Larisa Latynina performs on the balance beam at the 1960 Summer Games.

WOMEN'S OLYMPIC GAMES

Although women began competing in the Olympics early in the 20th century, they weren't initially allowed to participate in one of its most prestigious events: track and field. That led French athlete and activist Alice Milliat to start the Women's Olympic Games in 1922. The new competition was popular enough that the IOC allowed women to compete in track and field in the 1928 Summer Games in Amsterdam, the Netherlands.

Blankers-Koen had to fight against prejudices that many female athletes have often faced. She was often criticized for competing in sports rather than focusing on being a mom to her kids.

Soviet gymnast Larisa Latynina is one of the most decorated athletes of all time. She won 18 medals total in the 1956, 1960, and 1964 Games. That's more than any other female athlete, summer or winter. Nine of Latynina's medals were gold, including three in the floor exercise and two all-around victories. She's also one of only three women to win the same event three times in the Summer Olympics.

Latynina revolutionized gymnastics with her style and grace, and she raised the level of competition in the floor exercise with her artistic agility.

She was a friendly rival of teammate Polina Astakhova. The two Soviets are the only gymnasts to be part of three gold-medal-winning teams. Astakhova couldn't quite compete with Latynina's high medal count, but she won 10 in three Olympic Games from 1956 through 1964.

Agnes Keleti, a gymnast from Hungary, won 10 medals in the 1952 and 1956 Summer Olympics. She won five gold medals, three silver, and two bronze. She won four of her gold medals in 1956 in the floor exercise, uneven bars, balance beam, and team portable apparatus, which was similar to today's rhythmic gymnastics. She finished second to Latynina in the 1956 all-around competition.

Latynina wasn't the only female Olympian to win the same event three times. Australian swimmer Dawn Fraser did it, too. Known as one of the greatest female sprint swimmers of all time, Fraser won eight medals. She won the gold medal in the 100-meter freestyle in three straight Olympics. She was the first Olympic swimmer to win the same event three times. Fraser set world records in the

100 and the 4x100 relay and Olympic records in the 100 in 1960 and 1964. Her first Olympics was in her home country of Australia in 1956 when she was 18 years old.

Fraser was also the first woman to swim the 100 in under a minute, posting a time of 59.9-seconds on October 27, 1962. Australia named her the country's greatest female athlete in 1988. She was also named the "World Athlete of the Century" in 1999 at the World Sports Awards in Vienna, Austria.

Dawn Fraser was a trailblazing swimmer from Australia.

OVERCOMING OBSTACLES

Athletes have to rise above countless challenges before they can say they're Olympic champions. The female athletes of the 1960s and 1970s were no exception. Many of them proved that no hurdle is too high, no obstacle too great for a champion.

Wilma Rudolph started off on a pretty tough road. When she was four years old she contracted polio, a serious disease that can be crippling. Wilma wore leg braces until age 9. That's not the typical story for somebody who would become known as the world's fastest woman.

Wilma made the US track and field team for the 1956 Summer Games in Melbourne, Australia. She was just 16 years old. She won a bronze medal in the 4x100 relay, but that was just the beginning. Four years later in Rome, Italy, Rudolph became the first American woman to win three track and field gold medals in one Olympics. She won the 100- and 200-meter dashes and was part of the winning

Wilma Rudolph crosses the finish line at the 1960 Rome Olympics.

4x100 relay team. She also broke world records in all three events.

Gymnast Věra Čáslavská overcame political turmoil to shine at the 1968 Summer Games in Mexico City. She previously had won three events, including the all-around competition, at the 1964 Games in Tokyo, Japan. But after Soviet troops invaded her home country of Czechoslovakia in August 1968, Čáslavská was forced to spend three weeks living and training in the mountains. She made it to Mexico City, where she defended her all-around title and won three other gold medals.

A new gymnastics star emerged at the 1972 Summer Games in Munich, West Germany. The Soviet Union's Olga Korbut captivated fans with her daring moves. No one had ever done a backflip and caught herself on the uneven bars before Olga did it. In another new move, she sprung into a backward somersault on the balance beam.

Olga took home gold medals in the floor exercise, the balance beam, and the team competition. She won silver on the uneven bars. It was an amazing achievement. But an even younger gymnast would overshadow her in 1976.

Olga Korbut dazzled the judges at the 1972 Munich Games.

IMPROVISING PAYS OFF

The governments of Czechoslovakia and the Soviet Union weren't getting along in 1968. Vera Čáslavská's signed a document rejecting Soviet interference in her home country. After the invasion she decided to hide for her own safety. While living in the mountains for three weeks, she somehow managed to keep up her gymnastics training. She swung from the trees. She worked on her tumbling and floor routine. She found a way to stay in shape until the government allowed her to join her team in Mexico City for the Olympics. The practice paid off as she won six medals.

Nadia Comăneci was just 14 years old when she became the first female gymnast to earn a perfect 10 in an Olympic event. The Romanian teenager got a perfect score for her uneven parallel bar routine at the Summer Games in Montreal, Quebec. When the judges' scores were reported, the scoreboard showed "1.00." It took people in the arena a few seconds to realize that it meant Nadia had earned a perfect mark. The scoreboard wasn't built to display such a score.

Comăneci scored six more perfect 10s in Montreal and was the youngest all-around gold medalist ever. She also won gold in the uneven bars and balance beam.

Dorothy Hamill took home figure skating gold for the United States in 1976.

The other star of 1976 was US figure skater Dorothy Hamill, who won gold at the Winter Games in Innsbruck, Austria. Hamill's signature move was her innovative camel spin. Instead of simply keeping one leg in the air straight behind her, she bent her other leg and whirled into a sitting spin. People called it the "Hamill Camel."

Hamill's inspiration for the Olympics was US skater Peggy Fleming, who was part of an amazing comeback story. In 1961 the entire US figure skating team was killed in a plane crash while flying to an international competition. That thrust young skaters into the spotlight before many of them were ready. Fleming competed at the 1964 Winter Games when she was just 15 years old. She finished in sixth place. But she went back to work, and in 1968 Fleming won the Olympic gold medal in women's singles. She was the only US athlete to win a gold medal in the Winter Games that year.

Polish track and field athlete Irena Szewińska-Kirszenstein won seven medals in five Olympic Games (1964–1980). She competed in the 100-, 200-, and 400-meter dashes; the long jump; and the 4x100 relay. She also set 13 world records in her career, two in the Olympics.

Irena Szewińska-Kirszenstein sets a world record in the 400-meter dash at the 1976 Montreal Olympics.

CHAPTER 3

BREAKING RECORDS

The 1980s paved the way for an American gymnast to shine, a Soviet cross country skier to dominate, and track and field athletes to display speed and style.

Mary Lou Retton was the star of the 1984 Summer Olympics in Los Angeles, California. US athletes were favored in most events because the Soviet Union and many Eastern European countries boycotted the Olympics. But nobody was handing out medals. The athletes still had to earn them, and Retton did so, even though she was an unlikely candidate to break through.

Retton underwent knee surgery just five weeks before the Olympics. Her doctors didn't think she'd be able to compete. Also, Retton didn't look like the typical gymnast of that era. She was muscular and powerful, not petite and graceful.

But Retton proved the doctors and the doubters wrong at the Olympics. She scored perfect 10s in the floor exercise and vault. She beat her rival Ecaterina Szabo

Mary Lou Retton performs on the balance beam at the 1984 Los Angeles Games.

of Romania by 0.05 points to become the first American to win the all-around gold medal. Her five medals were more than any other athlete took home at those Los Angeles Games.

Katarina Witt performs in the women's figure skating final at the 1988 Winter Olympics in Calgary.

For years women battled the sentiment that their bodies were too delicate to endure long-distance running. Joan Benoit and her fellow runners put those fears to rest for good in 1984. Benoit won the gold medal in the first-ever women's Olympic marathon. A packed Los Angeles Coliseum roared as Benoit entered the stadium to complete the final lap of the historic race. She thrust both arms into the air as she broke the tape 400 meters ahead of her nearest competitor.

On ice in the 1980s, Katarina Witt was one of the greatest competitors of her era. She won gold medals in women's singles in 1984 and 1988, making her the first skater to defend her Olympic title since Sonja Henie in 1936. Witt was a natural with her sense of rhythm and graceful body for skating. And no woman had ever landed a triple flip in a competition until 1981, when she did it at the European Championships.

Witt wasn't the favorite to win gold in 1984. Many thought American Rosalyn Sumners would prevail. Witt was third early on in the competition but took the lead after the short program. Her bold skating performance in her German folk costume earned six first-place votes.

TENNESSEE STATE TIGERBELLES

Tennessee State University, a small, historically black college in Nashville, played a huge role in US women's track and field history. Ed Temple was the head coach of the Tigerbelles track program from 1950 to 1993. Over that span, the Tigerbelles produced 40 Olympic athletes. In 1960 all four runners in the 4x100 relay were from Tennessee State. His athletes—led by three-time gold medalists Wilma Rudolph and Wyomia Tyus—won 23 medals, 13 of them gold.

Witt returned in 1988 to beat out another American, Debi Thomas, in Calgary, Canada.

The first athlete to medal at five Olympic Winter Games was cross country skier Raisa Smetanina of the Soviet Union. She won a total of 10 medals, including four gold, from 1976 to 1992. That's a long time to compete and be successful in a sport. Her first Olympic appearance was probably her best. She won medals in all three of her races, with a silver and two golds. Smetanina didn't let age get in the way, either. She won her last gold medal as

Raisa Smetanina, shown here at the 1976 Winter Games, had an amazing Olympic career.

part of a relay team in 1992, only 12 days before her 40th birthday. She was the oldest female gold medalist ever.

US speed skater Bonnie Blair showed endurance and determination while winning five gold medals and a bronze over the four Olympics she competed in. She is the only woman to win the same Olympic speed skating event three times in a row. She won gold in the 500 meters in 1988, 1992, and 1994. Blair was unstoppable in that event, breaking the world record four times, including once at the Olympics. Russian Lidiya Skoblikova is the only athlete with more speed skating gold medals than Blair.

US track and field athlete Jackie Joyner-Kersee also had a long Olympic career. She won six medals over four Games from 1984 to 1996. Her specialties were the long jump and heptathlon. In all, she won two gold medals and a silver in the heptathlon. She's often called the best female athlete of all time.

Joyner's sister-in-law, Florence Griffith Joyner, shared some of the US track fame in this era. The sprinter set world records in the 100- and 200-meter dashes. After winning a silver medal in the 200 in Los Angeles in 1984,

Bonnie Blair races to the gold medal in the 500-meter race at the 1994 Winter Olympics.

she dominated the 1988 Summer Games in Seoul, South Korea. "Flo-Jo" took gold in the 100, 200, and 4x100 relay. Griffith Joyner broke the world record in the 200 twice in Seoul. She ran a 21.56 in the semifinals and a 21.34 in the final. In the same race, Jamaican Grace Jackson ran a 21.72. That would have been 0.01 seconds off the previous world record had Griffith Joyner not shattered it in the semifinals. Through 2016 no woman had surpassed Flo-Jo's 21.34 in the 200. Fellow American sprinter Marian Jones came the closest. Jones ran a 21.62 in 1998.

Nawal El-Moutawakel of Morocco was the first woman from an Islamic nation to win an Olympic gold medal. She won the 400-meter hurdles at the 1984 Summer Games in Los Angeles.

Nawal El-Moutawakel rejoices after winning her gold medal in 1984.

STARS AND SCANDALS

Athletes can inspire their teammates, their fans, or the whole nation when they fight through injuries to compete at the highest level. Some of the great stories of the 1990s revolved around great comeback stories.

Gymnast Kerri Strug was part of the "Magnificent Seven" US women's gymnastics team at the 1996 Summer Games in Atlanta, Georgia. The United States was in position to win the team gold medal, but first Strug had to compete on the vault. She had two chances. She needed to land on her feet once. Strug fell on her first attempt and twisted her left ankle in the process.

She limped and felt some pain, but she ran for her second vault anyway, with her coach Béla Károlyi cheering her on saying, "You can do it!" Strug stuck the second landing, practically on one foot, then quickly dropped to her knees in pain. Two ligaments in her left ankle were torn. But her second vault clinched the team gold

Kerri Strug winces after tearing ligaments in her ankle during a vault at the 1996 Atlanta Games.

medal for the Magnificent Seven, the first US women's gymnastics team to win gold.

Figure skater Nancy Kerrigan overcame an injury that unwittingly thrust her into the middle of one of the biggest scandals in sports history. Kerrigan and her US teammate Tonya Harding were on track to clash at the

Nancy Kerrigan, *right*, did her best to ignore the controversy surrounding Tonya Harding at the 1994 Lillehammer Games.

MAGNIFICENT MILLER

Shannon Miller is one of the most decorated gymnasts in history. As a 15-year-old, she won five medals in Barcelona in 1992, more medals than any other American athlete at those Olympics. She won silver in the all-around competition and balance beam, plus three bronze medals in team, floor exercise, and uneven bars. In 1996 Miller finally won gold as the leader of the Magnificent Seven. She also won gold on the balance beam in Atlanta.

1994 Olympics in Lillehammer, Norway. But less than two months before the Games began, after a practice in Detroit at the US Nationals and Olympic trials, Kerrigan was attacked. The assailant hit her on the right knee with a pipe, badly injuring her. Three people connected to Harding were arrested for the attack.

Kerrigan was able to compete in the Olympics. She won a silver medal, losing out on gold by just one tenth of a point to 16-year-old Oksana Baiul from Ukraine. Harding finished in eighth place. After the Olympics, Harding admitted her role in the attack, and she was banned from amateur skating for life.

Another American skating duo had a much different Olympic experience. Michelle Kwan went to the Lillehammer Olympics

when she was only 13 years old. She was only there to fill in if a teammate was injured, and she didn't get to skate in those Games. Michelle returned to the Olympics four years later in Nagano, Japan, as the reigning world champion. That made her the favorite to win the gold medal. She completed seven triple jumps and was careful not to have any technical errors. Michelle did well, but her 15-year-old teammate Tara Lipinski did a little better. Like Michelle, she did seven triples, but Tara added her special triple loop-triple loop combination and ended her program with a triple toe/half loop/triple Salchow sequence.

It was enough for Tara to become the youngest Olympic figure skating champion ever. Michelle won the silver.

Some Olympic careers are remarkable because they're so long. There's Dara Torres, a US swimmer who competed

Tara Lipinski listens to the US national anthem after winning the women's figure skating gold medal in 1998.

in five Olympics between 1984 and 2008. Torres is one of three Olympians to win at least four medals of each color, giving her 12 total. She appeared to be retired from swimming after the 1992 Summer Games in Barcelona, Spain. But Torres returned to the pool in 1998 and qualified for the 2000 Games in Sydney, Australia, where she won five medals.

Torres returned again eight years later in Beijing, China, where she was the oldest female Olympic swimmer ever at age 41. She won three silver medals in those Games.

US swimmer Dara Torres won three medals in the 2008 Beijing Games at age 41.

US SUCCESS

Olympic opportunities for women had nearly caught up to those for men by the dawn of the 21st century. And American women continued to shine on the world's biggest stage.

Gymnast Simone Biles was part of the US team in 2016 that dubbed itself the "Final Five." The name honored coach Martha Károlyi, who retired after the Olympics that year in Rio de Janeiro, Brazil. Gabby Douglas, Aly Raisman, Laurie Hernandez, and Madison Kocian pooled their talents with Biles. The United States won the team gold by the largest margin of victory at any international tournament since a new scoring

The US women's gymnastics team dominated the competition at the 2016 Rio Games.

system was introduced to gymnastics in 2006. Team USA beat Russia by 8.209 points.

Biles was the first US gymnast to win four gold medals at one Olympic Games. In addition to her team medal, Biles was the fourth US woman in a row to win the Olympic all-around title. She also won gold on the vault and floor exercise and took bronze in the balance beam.

Raisman and Douglas were also part of the gold-medal winning team in London

Canada's women's hockey team has dominated Olympic competition.

in 2012. Douglas was the all-around champion in London, while Raisman won the floor exercise. In Rio, Raisman finished runner-up to Biles in the all-around and floor exercise.

The Canadian women's hockey team won four of the first five gold medals after the event started in 1998. Canada won gold in 2002, 2006, 2010, and 2014, beating the United States in the finals three of the four times.

Before the Final Five, Shawn Johnson and Nastia Liukin carried the US gymnastics hopes in 2008 in Beijing. Liukin had followed in her parents' footsteps with her gymnastics success. Her father won two gold medals for the Soviet Union in 1988. Her mother was the rhythmic gymnastics world champion the year before.

Liukin was the all-around champion in Beijing. Her five medals at the Games tied her with Mary Lou Retton and Shannon Miller for the US gymnastics record of five medals at one Olympics. Meanwhile, 16-year-old Johnson took home a gold in the balance beam and three silvers.

The gym isn't the only place where the United States has dominated. The women have come through in the pool, too, shattering multiple records.

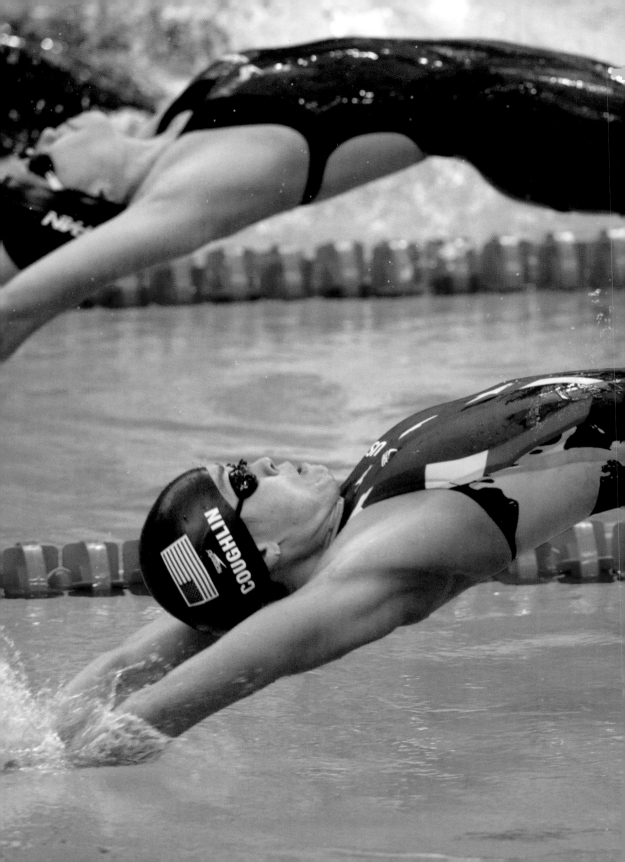

AGELESS WONDER

Olympic gymnasts usually have a short window for elite competition. Gymnasts typically are done by their early 20s, meaning they often compete in just one or two Olympics. Oksana Chusovitina from Uzbekistan is an exception. She competed at the Rio Games in 2016 as a 41-year-old. It was her unprecedented seventh Olympics. She's the oldest gymnast to compete in the Olympics. She won two medals, including a team gold in her first Olympics in 1992 and a silver in the vault in 2008.

American swimmer Natalie Coughlin won the gold medal in the 100-meter backstroke in 2004 and then again in 2008, becoming the first woman to defend her Olympic title in this event. Over three Olympics, Coughlin swam in 12 events and came away with 12 medals, including three golds. No Olympic athlete has ever entered more events and won a medal in each of them.

Missy Franklin followed in Coughlin's wake, breaking through as a 17-year-old at the 2012 London Games. She won four gold medals, including a sweep of the 100- and 200-meter backstroke races.

US swimmer Natalie Coughlin, *foreground*, was an all-time great in the backstroke.

American Katie Ledecky made her case as the greatest distance swimmer of all time. As a 15-year-old, Ledecky won the gold medal in the 800-meter freestyle at the London Games. Four years later she won four gold medals in Rio. She's most remembered for blowing away the competition in the 800, finishing 11 seconds before the silver medalist.

US swimmer Simone Manuel became the first black woman to win Olympic gold in the pool when she won the 100-meter freestyle event in Rio. She also won gold as part of the 4x100 medley relay team and took home two silver medals as well.

Meanwhile, the duo of Kerri Walsh Jennings and Misty May-Treanor formed the most dominant female beach volleyball team ever. They won gold medals in 2004, 2008, and 2012. They were truly unbeatable, winning all 21 of their Olympic matches. After the London Games in 2012, May-Treanor retired. But Walsh Jennings teamed with April Ross to win the bronze medal in Rio in 2016.

Kerri Walsh Jennings, *left*, and Misty May-Treanor discuss strategy during a match at the 2012 London Games.

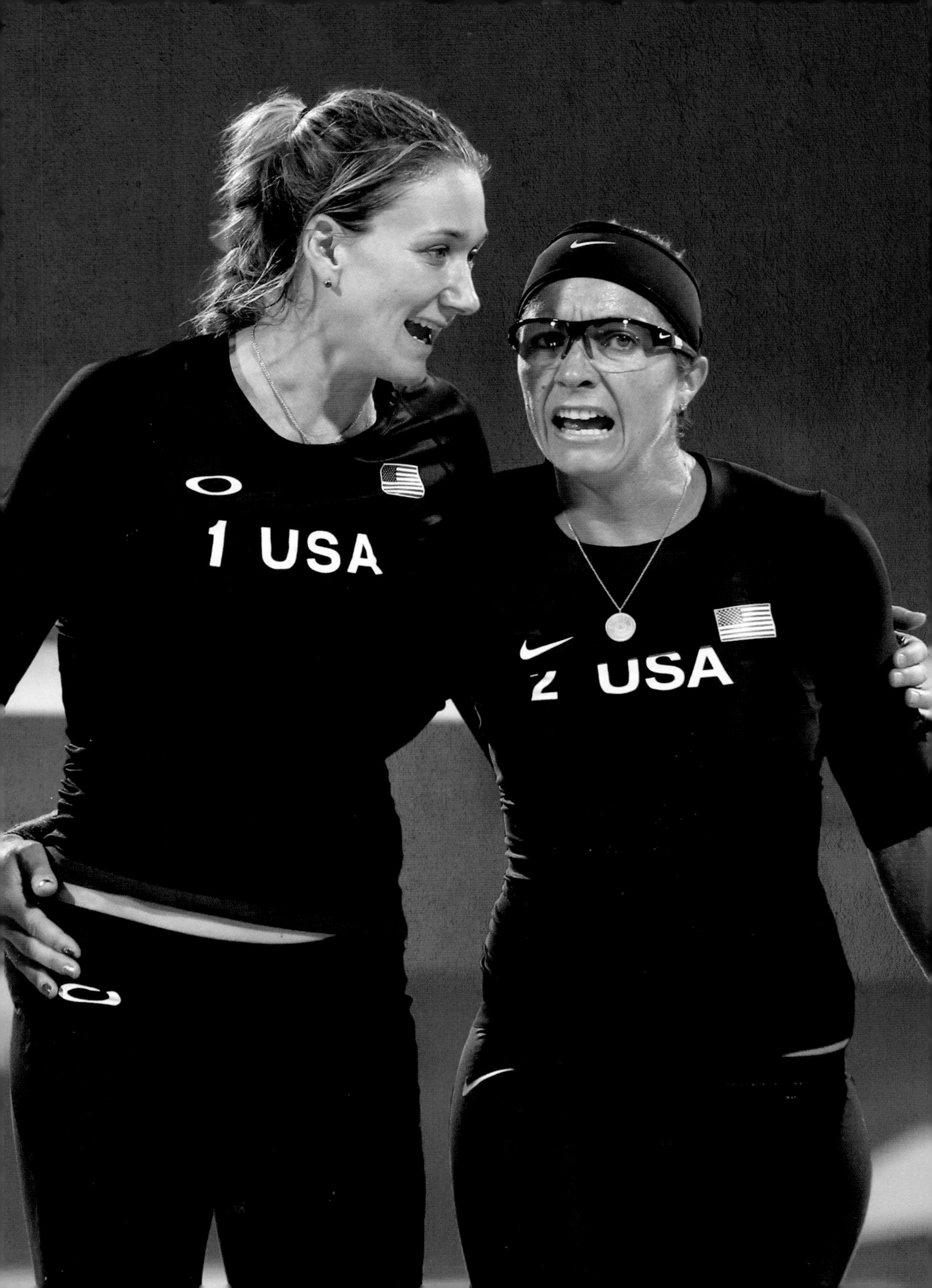
1 USA
2 USA

GLOSSARY

ERA
A period of time in history.

INJURY
Damage or harm, usually to one's body.

INVADE
To send armed forces into another country in order to take it over.

JUDGES
Officials who decide the results in some competitions.

MEDALIST
One who finishes in the top three of an event at the Olympics.

POLIO
An infectious disease that attacks the brain and spinal cord, often of young children.

RELAY
A race in which teammates take turns running or swimming laps.

REVOLUTIONIZE
To make sweeping changes.

RIVAL
An opponent with whom a player or team has a fierce and ongoing competition.

SCANDAL
A dishonest or immoral act that shocks people and disgraces those involved.

BOOKS

Anderson, Jennifer Joline. *Wilma Rudolph: Track & Field Inspiration*. Minneapolis, MN: Abdo Publishing, 2011.

Douglas, Gabrielle. *Raising the Bar*. Grand Rapids, MI: Zondervan, 2013.

Gray, Karlin. *Nadia: The Girl Who Couldn't Sit Still*. Boston, MA: Houghton Mifflin Harcourt, 2015.

WEBSITES

To learn more about women in sports, visit **abdobooklinks.com**. These links are routinely monitored and updated to provide the most current information available.

PLACE TO VISIT

Centennial Olympic Park
265 Park Ave. W NW
Atlanta, Georgia 30313
404-223-4412
www.gwcca.org/park/
Centennial Olympic Park is located in downtown Atlanta. It's a 21-acre park that serves as a lasting reminder of the 1996 Summer Games. The park is centrally located, surrounded by many landmarks of downtown Atlanta. One of the park's highlights is a fountain in the shape of the Olympic rings.

INDEX

ABOUT THE AUTHOR

Heather Rule is a writer, sports journalist, and social media coordinator. She has a bachelor's degree in journalism and mass communication from the University of St. Thomas in St. Paul, Minnesota.